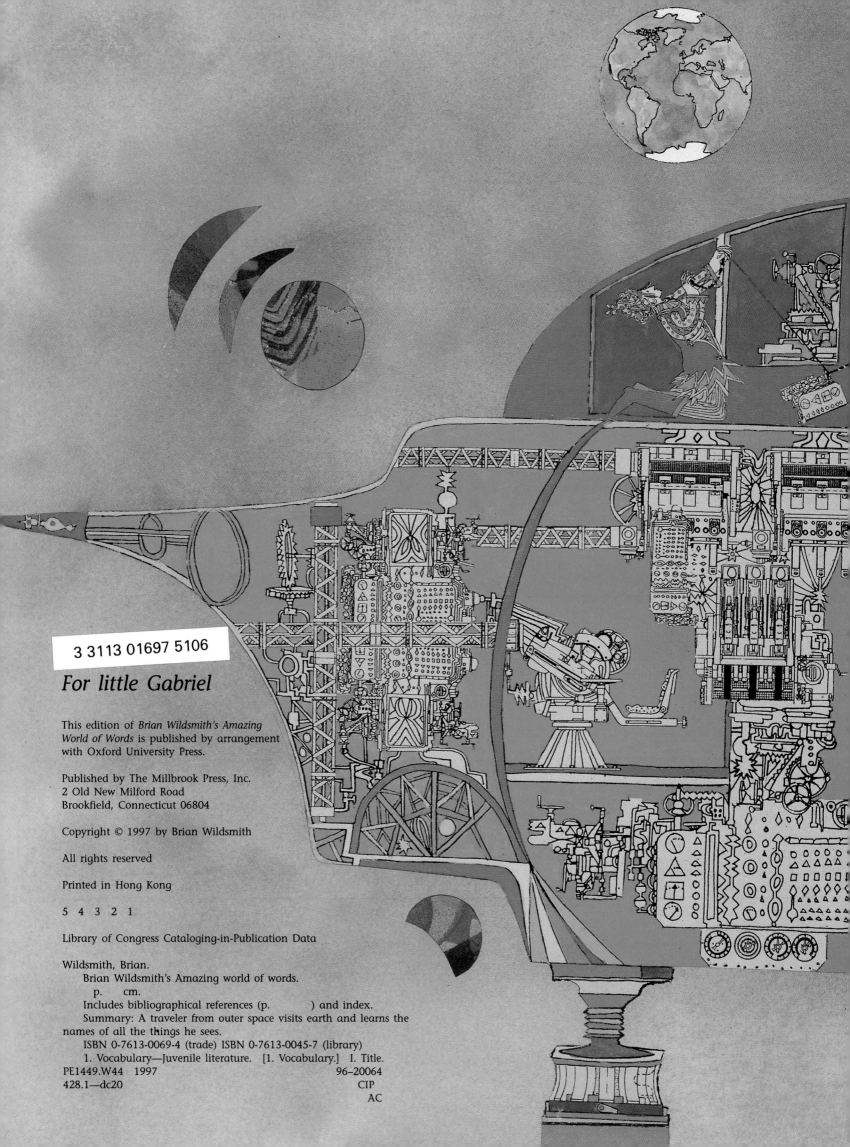

*For little Gabriel*

This edition of *Brian Wildsmith's Amazing
World of Words* is published by arrangement
with Oxford University Press.

Published by The Millbrook Press, Inc.
2 Old New Milford Road
Brookfield, Connecticut 06804

Printed in Hong Kong

5 4 3 2 1

Library of Congress Cataloging-in-Publication Data

Wildsmith, Brian.
    Brian Wildsmith's Amazing world of words.
        p.    cm.
    Includes bibliographical references (p.        ) and index.
    Summary: A traveler from outer space visits earth and learns the
names of all the things he sees.
    ISBN 0-7613-0069-4 (trade) ISBN 0-7613-0045-7 (library)
    1. Vocabulary—Juvenile literature.  [1. Vocabulary.]  I. Title.
PE1449.W44  1997                              96–20064
428.1—dc20                                    CIP
                                              AC

Brian Wildsmith's

# AMAZING WORLD OF WORDS

The Millbrook Press
Brookfield, Connecticut

shooting star

spaceship

planets

moon

satellite            sun            Earth            space capsule            astronaut

ancient ruins  pyramid  donkey  carpet  Bedouin  palm tree  horseman

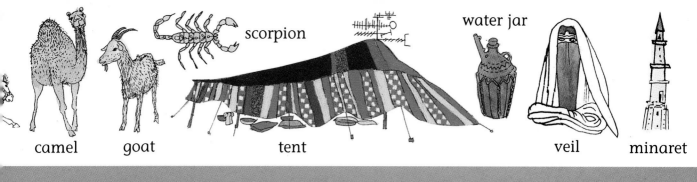

camel    goat    scorpion    tent    water jar    veil    minaret

puffer fish

fishing boat

sea horse

shark

seagull

shell

submarine

cra

whale

scorpion fish

jellyfish

ferry

submersible

seal

lighthouse

mountaineer

volcano

pylon

pleasure boat

clouds

lightni